Just Get Started

Just Get Started

Tips for Starting, Running, and Growing
Your Online Business

Copyright © 2014 by Ray Edwards

All rights reserved. Written permission must be secured from publisher to use or reproduce any part of this book, except for brief quotations in critical reviews or articles.

Designed by Sean Edwards
EdwardsPublishingHouse.com

Cover Design by Juan Lopez Design
JuanLopezDesign.net

Published in Spokane, Washington, by Ray Edwards International, Inc.

Ray Edwards International, Inc.
2910 E 57th Ave
Suite 5 #330
Spokane, WA 99223

RayEdwards.com

ISBN-13: 978-1500989590
ISBN-10: 1500989592

Table of Contents

About the Author i

What They Say About Ray iii

FREE Audio Seminar: Copywriting Quickstart v

Introduction: The Master Key to Success vii

1. How to Start Your Online Business 1
2. Fast & Easy List-Building 5
3. Do Product Launches Still Work? 7
4. 3 Simple Tactics to Build Your Email List Faster 11
5. Stop Struggling With Your Nature 15
6. What Is One Thing You Could Do Differently? 19
7. Why People Hate Marketers 21
8. Quit Working So Hard So You Can Get More Done 23
9. Weak Link in Your Selling Process? 31
10. Darth Vader's Mastermind Group 35
11. Teddy Roosevelt Business Secrets 37
12. Magic Power Gets Anyone to Do Anything 41
13. 78-Year Old Bank Teller Foils Robbery 45
14. What the Heck Is "Laughter Yoga"? 47
15. Dead Men Don't Blog 49
16. How to Become a Superhero 51
17. Simple But Not Easy 55
18. Mint.com, the "iPad" Business Lesson, and Toyota 57
19. 3 Keys to Instantly Make Your Business More Effective 61

20. "It Is What It Is": How to Handle Problems............................ 65
21. 7 Stupid Ways to Define Success 67
22. The A-Team School of Marketing 69
23. 3 Lies That Hold You Back 71
24. How to Write a Book in 7 Days.. 73
25. What Were You Put Here to Do? 77
26. BS Excuses That Kill Greatness 79
27. Tonight, We Try to Take Over the World................................. 83
28. 5 Fundamentals of Bulletproof Business Profits 85
29. Strength: the Secret Power of Achievement............................ 87
30. 7 Effortless Productivity Tips... 89
31. The Inception Guide to Marketing 91
32. Get Instant Value From Your Dusty Old Info-Products 93
33. There Are No Secrets 95
34. Marketing by Number 97
35. Are Your Internet Business Goals Too High?....................... 101
36. 3 Little Marketing Moves That Make More Money 105
37. What To Do Next 107

   How to Contact Ray... 109

About the Author

Ray Edwards is one of the world's highest-paid advertising copywriters and marketing/business coaches.

His sales copy and marketing advice are amazingly effective – having sold an estimated $100 million in products and services.

Ray's all-star list of clients includes New York Times best-selling authors Tony Robbins, Jack Canfield, and Mark Victor Hansen (creators of *Chicken Soup for the Soul*), Joel Comm (author of *Twitter Power, Ka-Ching,* and *The Adsense Code*), Robert Allen (author of *Nothing Down* and *Creating Wealth*), and Raymond Aaron (author of *Double Your Income Doing What You Love*).

Ray has written thousands of pages of copy–radio commercials, TV commercials, direct mail pieces, one-sheets, fliers, brochures, billboards, music-on-hold scripts, training manuals, corporate policy and procedures, web site copy, and email marketing campaigns.

He speaks frequently at seminars on copywriting, promotions, and marketing for professionals in those fields.

He has appeared in magazines, newspapers, trade journals, and on national radio and TV.

Ray is the author of the #1 best-sellers *Writing Riches, Money-Words,* and *The Ultimate Freelance Writer's Handbook.*

For more resources, a weekly Internet radio show (podcast), and to subscribe to Ray's FREE email newsletter, visit RayEdwards.com

What They Say About Ray

"He is generous with his teachings and holds nothing back."
– Joel Comm, New York Times best-selling author of *Twitter Power,* *Ka-Ching,* **and** *The Adsense Code*

"He is simply one of the best living copywriters today."
- Mike Filsaime

"Ray has written sales copy for some of the top Internet marketers, as well as other businesses… and not just one-time gigs… his clients come back to do business with him again and again. Why would they do that? Only one reason… because what he does gets results."
- Martin Howey, Owner, TopLine Business Solutions

"Ray Edwards is the master of direct response copywriting. The results of my working with him have literally catapulted me into the million dollar revenue makers in the direct response marketing industry."
- Jack Bosch, Orbit Investments

"Highest integrity, a pleasure to work with… and fantastic work. I love working with Ray."
- Jeff Walker, Creator of Product Launch Formula

FREE Audio Seminar: Copywriting Quickstart

Claim Your FREE Audio Seminar and Bonuses ...

- The *Copywriting Quickstart* **Audio Training** (secret formulas for speed copywriting)...
- **The one-page copywriting guide** (the basics of copywriting "at-a-glance")...
- **The one-page headline guide** (a quick "cheat sheet" for writing killer headlines)...

Claim your free training now...
RayEdwards.com/moneywords

Introduction

The Master Key to Success

How many times have you heard self-help or business gurus talk about how they 'uncovered' the 'real secrets' of success? Hundreds? Thousands? Right. Me too.

Well, let me save you some money and time. Forget the gurus for a moment. Here is the real, true, 'Master Secret of Success':

Just get started!

Don't laugh. The problem most business people, entrepreneurs, and companies have is that they spend far too much time coming up with new buzzwords and management systems – and almost zero time just getting down to the work that needs to be done.

For the individual or entrepreneur, I offer this tactic that will help you 'get started' on something that will generate new revenue...

Think carefully about your answer to this question:

If you could only do one thing to generate revenue immediately, what would that one thing be?

I really want you to think about this. If it was a "must"–for instance, if it meant being able to pay the mortgage on your house this month–what one thing would you do right now? Some possible examples:

- Write a letter and mail it.
- Make a phone call.
- Send an email.
- Drive to see a prospect in person.
- Complete and deliver a proposal.

Okay, do you have your "one thing"? Great. Write it down. Now... JUST GET STARTED!

When that is done, do the whole exercise over again.

I know that right about now you're thinking, "Ray, this is the most elementary, simple, stupid thing I've heard all week."

That's okay. Try it anyway–and after you have tried it, I'd love to hear from you with your success story.

And remember, you heard the Master Key to Success right here. In case you forgot already, it's this:

Just get started!

~ Just Get Started ~

1

How to Start Your Online Business

I hear from so many people who feel overwhelmed by the complexity of starting an online business.

There are only a few simple things you need to get started making money with your own Internet-based business. It's not complicated, really.

Let me break it down for you. I'll tell you the basic items you need, and Google can tell you the rest (just search for information on the areas where your knowledge is weak or incomplete).

Here's what you need:

1. A Product. Obviously, you need something to sell. This could be software, items you sell on eBay, a service, or an information product.

People get hung up on how to come up with a product.

The truth is that products are the easiest thing in the world to get. It's taking action that's tough.

2. A Domain Name. This seems obvious, but you need a name for your business. You can get one for about $10 a year.

3. A Web Page. I say "page" instead of "site," because a "site" seems complicated. A "page" sounds easy, doesn't it? You can get one for about $70 a year.

4. Web Page Software. You need to build a page with content on it. You can do it yourself with free software from http://nvu.com, or you can use a paid product like Dreamweaver (which is available at http://www.adobe.com).

5. Graphics. You need a logo and a "look and feel" for your products or services. Again, you can use free software (like that at http://www.gimp.org) or you can buy something like Photoshop, which you will find at the Adobe site (http://www.adobe.com).

6. An Auto-Responder Account. This is an account that allows you to build a mailing list so that you can mail to your customers or prospects.

It can also do this for you on an automated sequential basis, so once someone signs up they get an email from you on a regular basis automatically.

7. Shopping Cart Software. You need to be able to take payments somehow, right? My advice is to get a nice, proven, all-in-one solution.

You can get my current recommendations for each of these tools by going to RayEdwards.com/resources.

Now, each of these is a somewhat complex discussion and we could probably spend several chapters talking about each of them. Do a quick search on Google–there are plenty of online resources that will teach you more about each of these subjects.

You now know the basic building blocks needed to build your online business.

Can you spend years learning to master it all? Yes. But it is simple enough to get the basics in just a few minutes (as you just did).

Don't let yourself get overwhelmed. Just remember these 7 basics, figure out which pieces you already have... and figure out what the next logical step would be. Then just do it!

2

Fast & Easy List-Building

I get a lot of questions asking how to build a list and do it quickly. Actually, it's a lot easier to build a list than you might think.

The fact is the techniques of list-building are really quite simple. These three tactics will help you to build your list quickly:

Use a "squeeze page"

I find that, while everyone seems to know about the effectiveness of a squeeze page, few are actually doing it, or if they are, they're not using a true squeeze page.

You must admit, it takes a little bit of backbone to say, "You don't get to see anything until you give me your e-mail address!"

I promise you, though, if you use a squeeze page you'll get subscribers, and you'll build your list.

If you look at my squeeze page for Ray Edwards Copywriting, you'll see that I don't even offer an ethical bribe to get people to opt in, yet my conversion rate for this page is about 38 %.

Do "ad swaps" with other list owners

Look for people with ads in their e-zines, contact them and say,

"Hey, I have an e-zine, too! How about we trade ads?" Then, you run an ad for their list and they run an ad for your list.

If they don't offer ads (or you don't offer ads), simply contact them and say, "I would like to promote your email newsletter to my subscribers; would you do the same for me?"

In your e-mail newsletter, then, you just add a little paragraph that says, "I've discovered a great newsletter that I think you'd enjoy. Here's the link."

This, by the way, is one of the best and fastest ways to build your list. I know, it's too easy. But it works.

Look for opt ins through forum postings

You can post good content to forums. Many forums will allow you to add text to your signature line.

Try something simple, like "To get my 'Seven Tips on List-Building,' click here." That link leads readers directly to your opt-in page.

Make sure you have a decent ethical bribe to offer–a special report, audio clip, video clip, a PDF file, or even free software.

Don't subscribe to any forums? Now may be the time to start! All you need is twenty minutes a day. Use that time to check out ten forums, add quality posts, answer any questions, and include your signature line link.

This really works–I get new subscribers every day from this method, and I don't even have time to post to forums anymore.

3

Do Product Launches Still Work?

You may be wondering if product launches "still work." Marketers ask this question all the time. Everyone knows how to do it (or more accurately stated: they think they know how to do it), but is it still worth doing?

Using product launches is a great strategy: one that works as well as ever. However, the "standard" product launches aren't producing the same results that they did a year ago.

By "standard," I mean: copying only the externally obvious tactics, and neglecting the psychological triggers that make launches so effective. The only person I know of who teaches those triggers is the guy who invented the whole idea: Jeff Walker.

To make a successful product launch now, you need to follow a formula. Let's face it, all the low-hanging fruit has already been picked. But with this formula, created by Jeff Walker, you can have a successful product launch.

You may have heard of the Membership Site Bootcamp launch. Jeff was the quarterback for that launch (I wrote much of the copy), which created $1.7 million in the first week!

So, yes, product launches are still an effective way to create a profit windfall.

I encourage you to check out Jeff's Product Launch Formula.

Even if you don't plan on purchasing his course, he still gives away great free information on his site.

Here are three tactics you can use to boost launch results:

Tactic #1: Use a "Reverse squeeze page"

This term was created by John Reese, I believe, and not too long ago at that.

In this case, you offer free content before you ask for their opt-in information.

As an example, you offer them a free article or video. At the end, advise clients that you will be creating more of the same.

"If you'd like to get more videos absolutely free, fill in your name and e-mail address."

In this case, you give something to get something.

Tactic # 2: Give them your best material up front, for free

No, I'm not crazy. When I suggest this, the most common response is, "But if I give them my best stuff for free, there won't be anything to sell them!"

In fact, this is not a problem. The great copywriter Eugene Schwartz, author of *Breakthrough Advertising*, pioneered this method, and it works!

He found that when you gave away something terrific, people's perceived value of your other products increases. Readers think, "WOW! If this is what they give away for free, their other stuff must be incredible!"

So what happens if they get into your site and find that your product isn't as good as the stuff you gave away free?

That's when you benefit from the "Halo Effect." People will be amazed by your great freebies and so credit your saleable material as being better than it may actually be. It takes no manipulation on your part.

Tactic #3: Share your story with your sublist

Don't e-mail them to tell them that you're going to sell to them ("watch your email Monday!"). That's not a story–it's a statement. People love stories.

Offer them personal insights into the business, tell them how the launch is progressing, or take them to blog posts. Use all the principles of influence that Jeff teaches in his course. It's worth it!

I highly recommend Jeff's Product Launch Formula and think it's a wise investment.

If you can't get it right now, use these three tips for your next product launch. You'll improve your conversions and get more business.

4

3 Simple Tactics to Build Your Email List Faster

Lately, Internet marketers have been telling me, "Ray, people don't opt in to squeeze pages nowadays. They just don't opt in like they used to."

Do remarks like this have you nodding in agreement?

Fear and paranoia, with a healthy dose of spam, have made it harder to get people to opt in.

At one time, it was so easy. All you had to do was add a form that said, "Sign up here to get e-mails," and the world would flock to your site.

People would opt in like crazy! E-mails, e-newsletters – everything was so new and exciting. My, how things have changed!

Today, we are deluged with e-mails. People are constantly changing e-mail addresses. People have multiple e-mail addresses–heck, some people even have a fake e-mail address that they never check, just to deal with all the spam. Cutting through the clutter is a challenge.

How can you make sure you are getting real opt-ins from people who will actually read the e-mails you send out?

There are ways to increase your opt-in conversions. These simple ideas don't take a lot of work, but they are very effective.

Try these three ideas to boost your opt-ins:

1. Make a stronger offer

We all know you have to give an ethical bribe to get people to opt in: a special report, an audio, a video, a piece of software.

If you just say, "Sign up to get my newsletter," to the average reader that means, "Sign up so I can spam you." You need to be more creative.

Work harder to create a better premium to offer your subscribers. If you're offering a special report, it better be a killer special report and not the same old crap that everybody else is offering.

You need to come up with a unique angle, and it needs to be well-written. Same is true of audio, video or software. It needs to be well done. It needs to be unique, something obtainable only through you, and it needs to address a need that is in line with the desires of your readers.

2. Use a hybrid subscription button

Go to my website RayEdwards.com, and look at the button on the subscription forms.

If you are signed into your Facebook account, you can register for my email list simply by clicking the blue Facebook button. If you are not signed into your Facebook account, there is a simple email subscription form featuring a green subscription button.

Notice that it's larger than most buttons you see on subscription forms. It's no accident that we chose green is the color of the button. That is a subtle, psychological hint that takes people from "Stop" to "Go!"

Yeah, that's a little silly, but in my experience, it increases conversions.

This intelligent button that changes depending on whether or not you are signed into Facebook is a "hybrid" subscription button. It adapts to the state of the visitor. My recommendation is that you try this kind of button too.

3. Keep distractions off your opt-in pages

The best opt-in pages are very clean and simple. There are no distractions to take attention away from the opt-in option.

While these suggestions seem very simplistic, they really work. Try them for yourself, and watch your opt-in rates soar!

5

Stop Struggling With Your Nature

Have you ever noticed that over the years, you tend to do pretty much the same things?

What I mean is, if you're a reader you remain one, if you're a writer you tend to write, if you're a procrastinator you tend to keep procrastinating, and so forth.

I think one of the real tricks of success is to simply recognize these things you tend to do, and then find ways to make these tendencies support your success.

In fact, I believe most people are miserable because they fail to do just that. Instead of working with their tendencies in order to succeed (almost effortlessly), they identify their tendencies as the problem and vow to change.

That, my friend, is called swimming against the flow of the river. And while you may get credit for working your tail off while doing it, you're not going to make much progress relative to the shoreline.

Case in point: for the longest time I was worried about my information addiction.

And make no mistake... I am an info-addict.

In one morning, I read the six magazines I bought the day before, read part of a book, checked out the over 1,000 new items in Google Reader, watched a brilliant little video by Ed Dale over at the Thirty

Day Challenge site, and sifted through 52 emails (it was early, and it was the day after a US holiday, so email was light this particular morning).

I have dozens of PDFs in my "To Read" folder on my Macbook Pro. I have dozens more videos and audios to go through in my "To Listen" and "To Watch" folders.

And once upon a time I thought something was wrong with me because of this kind of behavior. So I struggled against it.

I read books about it. I read articles about it. I listened to self-help material about it. Is anyone other than me seeing the irony yet?

One day I stumbled across an article by Dan Kennedy in which he detailed his working habits... and I was shocked to discover they were identical to mine (at least when it came to information consumption)! Dan saw it not as a weakness to be changed... but rather as a strength to be nurtured.

That was life-changing for me. It gave me a way to stop struggling against my natural tendencies, and to embrace the way God made me.

That tendency to process large quantities of unrelated information allows me to form connections between ideas, concepts, and methods that I would not possess if I limited my intake of information.

Now I structure my work and my routine in such a way that my behavior in this regard is strengthened, reinforced, and nurtured – and then put to profitable use in my writing.

I look for ways to channel that stream of information so that it's not wasted.

For instance, I found an excellent piece by Chris Brogan on focused blogging recently. You can bet I will be implementing many of Chris's suggestions in my own routine.

Another source of inspiration and information on effective ways to channel my own natural tendencies is at the blog of my new friend Brian Clark (we met in Vegas at a blogging / marketing get-together).

Brian's site, Copyblogger, is an excellent resource no self-respecting copywriter or blogger should ignore.

Stop Struggling With Your Nature

So what does this all mean to you?

In my experience, it means that if you find yourself fighting the same old battles (chronic lateness, procrastination, forgetfulness), you've probably unwittingly been holding yourself back by resisting your own gifts.

If you have trouble with authority, why work in a job when it's clear you'd be happier as an entrepreneur?

If you are always late for appointments, why not just stop making appointments (Arnold Schwarzenegger reportedly refuses to make appointments with anyone, and he seems to be doing okay running the state of California)?

If you have tendencies that are frowned upon by others – for instance, sleeping during the day and staying up all night – why not look for a way to turn the tendency into an asset, for instance, by working via Internet with clients or companies in a different time zone... where suddenly YOU are the early riser?!

Just because certain tendencies, behaviors and attitudes are not "acceptable" in one context does not mean those qualities are "bad."

It simply means – at least in my experience – you need to find a different context! And that decision – how you live your life – is for most of us, entirely a choice.

To ward off the inevitable objections to my premise: yes, I recognize that there are behaviors and "tendencies" that are illegal, immoral, and unethical. That's not what we're talking about here. Anything that falls into those three categories should be jettisoned from your life. Enough said on that.

Now take a moment to think about this...

In what ways could your "Limiting tendencies" become strengths?

How could your rearrange your life to make it so? If you can find positive, proactive ways to answer those questions, you just might find yourself more productive, profitable, and happy.

6

What Is One Thing You Could Do Differently?

There's a lot of talk these days about the economy and what to do about it. In the world of business, there's a lot of talk about what businesses and entrepreneurs can do about the economy.

That might be such a broad topic that it isn't helpful. What might be more helpful: what can you do differently? You: One person.

You see, there is no such thing as One Economy. There are individuals who each have their own personal economy.

When those individuals move in concert on a mass scale (such as selling their stock because they're afraid, or reigning in their spending for the same reason), we see the effect and call it "The Economy."

What seems a more useful question might be:

What is one thing you can do differently that will have a positive effect on your personal economy?

Just pick one thing. Then do it. My contention: it's impossible to take a positive action on an individual level without that action affecting others.

If enough people do one thing differently... and that one thing is positive... and that one thing creates value... what happens to the mass results in what we call The Economy.

And looking back, ask yourself: what happened when a mass number of individuals did lots of little "one things" that were not positive, and that did not add value, such as borrowing too much money, cutting corners on quality, and failing to add value in every transaction?

Is it possible this is how we got into our current situation to begin with?

So... What one positive thing can you do differently today?

7

Why People Hate Marketers

People hate marketers because marketers lie, cheat, and steal.

Now, you may protest. You may say you don't lie, cheat, or steal. I understand. You adhere to the letter of the law, you follow the rules, and you resent the implication of any dishonesty.

But even if you are "clean" as a marketer, guess what? It doesn't matter. You see, what matters is if your customers think you lie, cheat, and steal, it might as well be true. Because it's true for them, and that's all that matters.

Perception is reality

What do you do then to change things? Change things. Be more than just "clean." Be honest. Not just to the letter of the law: be honest to the point that it makes you uncomfortable. Be refreshingly honest.

Think of Southwest Airlines. People love this airline, even though it has the most degrading boarding process of all airlines, it has the least amount of service offered in-flight, and has the highest percentage of screaming babies and inexperienced travelers.

So why do people love Southwest? Simple: they have been refreshingly honest about what they offer, so our expectations are always met.

Grit your teeth and ask: in what ways can you be refreshingly honest with your customers?

8

Quit Working So Hard So You Can Get More Done

Most of us work too hard to really get anything done.

There are many studies that demonstrate that multimillion dollar CEOs spend less than 30 minutes per day doing the work they're actually paid to do.

Why is this? It's because the higher we go in our levels of responsibility (and this is especially salient for entrepreneurs), the more likely it is we will be interrupted throughout the day by concerns, people, and tasks that are urgent. Things that need high-level attention from the entrepreneur, CEO, or manager, but that are not necessarily important.

This applies even if you are a freelance worker (or perhaps you started your own online business in your "spare time").

The key to success on a massive scale is to focus on revenue-generating activities as much as possible. Here's how you do that...

Focus on Revenue Generation

If you were to analyze your day, you would no doubt discover that less than 20% of your daily activity produces 80% or more of your total revenue.

Another way of looking at this is to realize that 80% of what you do doesn't really contribute to your income in a directly measurable way.

You may be familiar with this as Pareto's Law:

> **"80% of the results typically come from only 20% of the activity"**

Instead of expending a lot of effort trying to change that 20% number to a higher percentage, say 50 or 60%, it might be more useful to consider simply eliminating the 80%.

Sound almost impossible? In fact, you already know how to do this...

Day before Vacation Phenomenon

Have you ever experienced "the day before vacation phenomenon"?

You know what I'm talking about. You're leaving for vacation on, let's say, Thursday. Have you ever noticed how that Wednesday becomes the most efficient work day you've had in many weeks, perhaps months?

Have you noticed how, on the day before vacation starts, you get 10 times the work done in a single day?

You've probably also noticed the wonderful euphoric feeling you experience when you walk out of the office on that day. How you feel that everything is in its place, each task is handled, each responsibility delegated to a team member, or at the very least deferred until you get back.

On those days, don't you feel more at peace, in control, and effortlessly productive than on 99% of the other days of the year?

So there it is: your proof that you're actually capable of eliminating the 80% of normal time wasting, revenue depressing, stress inducing activity that makes up most of your days.

Dan, the "No Email Man"

I have a colleague named Dan who doesn't do e-mail. I don't mean that he does "very little" e-mail... I mean he doesn't do e-mail at all. He doesn't have an e-mail address!

Dan also doesn't have a cell phone. If you want to talk to Dan, you have to call him at his office. His phone is answered by his assistant who deftly protects Dan from time-wasting phone calls and appointments.

In fact, Dan has very few appointments. Yet he is very productive, very receptive and open to talking with people, and runs a multimillion dollar business.

He somehow manages to do it while living a sane, orderly, and peaceful life. So what excuse do the rest of us have?

My 3-Month Experiment

Just a few weeks ago, I wrapped up a three-month experiment. For three months, my wife and I traveled the United States in our motor home.

We ran our business in our "spare time" from that motor home using laptops, Wi-Fi Internet connections, and UPS stores.

While I will admit it was challenging at times, I can also tell you that on average for that three- month period, I worked about three hours a day on weekdays. Normally, my work day is anywhere from 8-10 hours long.

It was startling to realize that I could maintain (actually not just maintain, but increase) my net income while working around one-third fewer hours.

Now that I'm back in my "normal" environment, I am remaining very conscious of how much time I spend working versus how much time I spend "being busy," giving the APPEARANCE of work.

You see, I already know it's possible to maintain my income working only three hours a day. I should be clear here: some days are 12-hour days, and some days are zero-hour days.

It still averages out to three hours per day. It's never as neat as exactly 180 minutes each day. But the point is: what on earth have I been doing with those other 7-9 hours each day?

How about you? What could you do with an extra 7-9 hours of discretionary time every single day? Think about that.

Going Cold Turkey

Recently, I decided to experiment with my colleague Dan's lifestyle.

My wife and I got in our motor home once again and drove about six hours to a lake in Oregon. We visited a state park... where there is no Internet service and no cell phone signal. That meant I wasn't able to "sneak in" an e-mail scan, or send out a "tweet" on Twitter.

Going cold turkey was interesting. The first day I was a bit jittery. I experienced some "withdrawal" symptoms.

The second day I experienced a feeling of relaxation I haven't felt in a very long time.

By the third day, I was ready to continue the experiment for another two or three months; however, it was time to come back home!

These "free days," as Dan Sullivan calls them, are days where you have absolutely no contact with anything work related (cell phone, voicemail, Internet, files, business reading, etc.).

In my experience, "free days" have almost magical powers to renew and revitalize your spirit, body and mind.

Since getting back from my three-day "Cold Turkey" experiment, I've been more productive or energetic and more efficient than I have been for a long time.

So those "free days" are now on my calendar every single week; Friday through Sunday are work-free zones.

Having this space to let my mind unwind, to let my spirit relax, allows me to bring back more creativity, energy, and enthusiasm to the work I do Monday through Thursday.

I benefit, my family benefits, and my clients and their customers all benefit.

Try Your Own Experiment

So what does all this mean to you? After all, you may or may not have the luxury of spending three months puttering around the USA in your motor home (we were very blessed by God in being allowed such a privilege).

You may also find it seemingly impossible to take three days a week "off." But certainly you could take a single day, couldn't you?

After all, most of the major spiritual traditions of the world include some form of the "day of rest."

I think that is for a very important reason: we were designed to require such a day of rest each week.

So this week–just for this one week–take a single day that is totally free from any work. For that 24-hour period, put yourself on a diet where you don't take in any e-mails, Twitter messages, voicemails, cell phone calls, meetings or work of any kind.

You'll be forced to find other things to do. Some suggestions that might help you:

- Take a long walk with someone you love

- Spend some time over coffee talking

- Go see a play or movie, read a good (non-work-related) book

- Play a game

- Go visit an old friend or loved one

While this kind of "slowing down" might be difficult for some of us, I believe the benefits are extraordinary. But don't take my word for it.

Try it and see for yourself.

An Advanced Experiment

If you are "all in" for taking a single day off in the next week, perhaps you'd also like to try the advanced part of the experiment.

Two ways we fill that 80% of wasted time each week are in doing things that we either (a) don't like to do or (b) are not good at doing.

My "advanced experiment" is to choose three of those things (things you either don't like to do or that you are not good at) and find someone else to do them for you.

Your three items that you are going to "delegate" or "outsource" could be small and insignificant, or they could be large and important items.

They could be as simple as dusting the bookshelves, or as complex as creating the project plan for a major new initiative in your company. That's up to you. I'm only asking you to follow some simple directions:

1. **Pick something that** you're either not good at or that you don't like to do. And if you want extra credit, pick something that fits both of those criteria.

2. **Pick something that** definitely falls in the "80 percentile group," something that is not directly revenue producing for your company or your business.

3. **Pick three such** "somethings."

4. **Select someone else** to take care of these three tasks on your behalf.

5. **It can be someone** you know personally, who does it simply as a favor to you; it can be someone on your staff to whom you assigned the task; or you can "outsource" the task to someone in another state (or even on another continent) using the Internet.

Quit Working So Hard So You Can Get More Done

It doesn't really matter who you get to take care of it; it simply matters that it isn't you.

Try your own experiment (as outlined above).

9

Weak Link in Your Selling Process?

Every piece of your website is a link in the sales chain.

Each link leads to the next, and at the end of the chain are the sale and profits for you and your business.

We all know any chain is only as strong as its weakest link

One way to get a quick sales boost is: find the weak or broken links in your sales process and strengthen or repair them.

Almost every website has at least a few weak or broken links. I'm not just talking about hyperlinks, here... I'm talking about any crucial part of the sales process.

No website is perfect – no website is ever optimized fully. There's always room for improvement. In most websites I look at for clients, there are some basic fixes that can pay off in a big way.

Here are three examples of things you might want to do on your own website:

- **Fix Broken Links.** The most obvious example is actual broken links. These are frustrating at best for your visitors, and for many it will kill the sale instantly. Customers think "if they can't get their links fixed, what must their product be like?"

- **Remove Inconsistencies.** In the world of direct mail, there's a proven response boost when the message on the outside of the envelope matches the message on the headline of the letter inside.

- **Remove "Mind Stoppers."** Some things just cause us to "stop our mind" when reading a website.

The reason this is so is that we are wired to respond positively to consistency. We like getting what we expect. Even seemingly small inconsistencies send a subconscious signal to your prospects that all is not right.

Some specifics things to look for:

1. **Different typefaces or** look & feel on your pages.

2. **Lack of consistent** layout from one section of your site to the next.

3. **Jarring differences between** your major sales pages (opt-in page, sales letter page, order page, thank-you page). Get fanatical about consistency.

For example, strange or unnatural wording can cause us to stop in the flow of reading and ask "What? Huh?"

Even though these "Mind Stoppers" may only cause a pause of 1 or 2 seconds, they interrupt the flow of your sales message.

Avoid "Mind Stoppers" at all costs. The best way to find them: read your copy aloud, to another human being, in a natural tone and at an easy pace. Then have them read it aloud back to you.

In each case, mark any section that causes you to pause or stumble. Re-write those sections and remove the "Mind Stoppers."

Weak Link in Your Selling Process?

When you forge stronger links in your "Sales Chain," you'll increase your sales results.

And that means more profits for you and your small business.

10

Darth Vader's Mastermind Group

What good is a "mastermind group"? Ask Darth Vader. For almost a DECADE we all thought Darth was the villain of Star Wars.

And after more than 20 years in the making, the series of movies in the Star Wars saga tells the whole story.

Darth Vader started out as a good guy. He got off track. WAY off track. Then, in the end, he did the right thing. In the end, it turns out he was STILL a good guy.

Why? Because people in his Mastermind Group–the Jedi–got him back on the right path, even if it WAS at the last possible moment.

Between the training that Darth got from Obi-Wan...

...and the example his former master set for him...

...and the direct appeals of his son Luke...

Darth did the right thing and killed the Emperor.

He saved his son... the Rebellion... and his own soul.

That's what a Mastermind Group–a good one–will do for you. They will tell you what you're doing wrong, even when you're completely full of your own crap. Even when you think you're about to Rule the Universe.

> **The moment you start believing your own bull is usually the moment when you're about to take a big fall**

QUESTION: who do you have in YOUR life who's willing to tell you that you're about to "blow it"?

If you don't have somebody who's willing and committed to doing that, you need to find them–pronto.

There are several ways to do it. For instance, you can set up your own Mastermind Group. Find the members, recruit them, and set up the meetings, etc. It'll take some legwork, but it's worth the effort.

You could also join an existing small group, but good ones are hard to find and harder to get into. Just make sure you're not getting yourself into a negative gossip group that is PRETENDING to be a true "Mastermind." You'll know pretty quickly.

You can also pay to join a Mastermind.

This is often a good option, because the fact that there are "membership dues" helps weed out the people who are not such a good fit.

Whatever you do, make sure you get yourself involved in some kind of "Mastermind group." If it can save Darth Vader... what can it do for you?

11

Teddy Roosevelt Business Secrets

I recently read a book about Teddy Roosevelt. I want to share something with you I read from President Roosevelt.

Stick with me, Hoss–it's worth it.

If you've ever been falsely accused...if you've ever had anyone spread lies or deceit about you... celebrate!

Vocal critics are sending you a signal...the signal is: you're on the right track.

Don't take my word for it–here's what Theodore "Teddy" Roosevelt had to say about critics:

> "It is not the critic who counts; not the man who points out how the strong man stumbles, or where the doer of deeds could have done them better.

> "The credit belongs to the man who is actually in the arena, whose face is marred by dust and sweat and blood; who strives valiantly; who errs, who comes short again and again...who spends himself in a worthy cause; who at the best knows in the end the triumph of high achievement, and who at the worst, if he fails, at least fails

while daring greatly, so that his place shall never be with those cold and timid souls who neither know victory nor defeat."–Theodore Roosevelt

Now don't get me wrong. I'm talking about UNJUST criticism. I'm assuming you're doing good things, with right intentions, and you're being honest and fair in your dealings. If you're doing BAD things, you have bigger problems than being criticized.

So let's say you're creating value. You're being honest and fair. And then for some reason–WHAMO! Somebody you never even met starts criticizing you. Congratulations!

The only reason you're a target for these trouble-making complainers is... you're DOING something.

Most people never do ANYTHING… Especially the critics

In fact, in my mind, the letters of the word "C.R.I.T.I.C." actually stand for:

C–an't

R–eally

I–nvent

T–hings

I–nstead

C–riticizes

Rest assured the only way to be sure you're never criticized is: don't do anything. CERTAINLY, if you're having any success at all, you're going to get criticism. Welcome it.

Remember the business twist on all this that President Roosevelt certainly understood:

Your place "Shall never be with those cold and timid souls who knew neither victory nor defeat."

12

Magic Power Gets Anyone to Do Anything

As marketers and entrepreneurs, we have a simple job: Get other people to do what we want them to do

I'll leave the discussion about the ethical side of this for another time; let's just assume that you and I will always work for the best interests of our customers and prospects.

We want to get people to do what we want. It will help them. It will help us. But exactly how do we do it? There is a tactic that is almost magical:

The power of persuasion

You can, quite simply, get practically anyone to do practically anything. It's so simple you'll be tempted to shrug it off. Don't.

Take just a moment to think about the fact that you already know this works, because you already know people who have this power.

Don't you know at least one person who seems to be able to persuade people on just about any issue? Don't you know at least one person who can seemingly "sell ice to the Eskimos"?

So how is it that some people are able to do that – and more importantly, how can you do the same? Wouldn't that make an enormous impact on your business? Here is the big secret...

> **"Enter the conversation already taking place in your prospect's mind."**

As far as I know, that idea originated with the late, great copywriter Robert Collier.

If you can "join up" with what your prospects are already feeling and thinking, get in sync with them, and get them to identify you as "friendly" in a hostile world... they will listen to what you have to say.

Think of it this way: the easiest way to influence someone is with whatever is already influencing them.

It's a simple principle, but not easy to do. Here are some tips that will help you harness this seemingly magic power:

1. **Listen.** Pay attention to what people say.

2. **Hang out in** online forums. Track trends on Twitter. Collect the words, phrases and ideas your market uses. Speak back to them in their own words.

3. **Watch what people** do.

4. **Be conscious of** what your store or website visitors actually do. What causes them to opt in? To opt out? To buy? To ask for a refund?

5. **Nothing teaches like** behavior. People vote with their feet. Watch their feet.

6. **Think.** How can you solve their problems?

7. **How can you** solve them quickly... easily... and with simplicity? Be the "aspirin for their headache"–and abundance will be yours.

Magic Power Gets Anyone to Do Anything

If you can do these things, your readers/visitors/ listeners will be nodding their heads, slapping the tabletop, and saying, "Yes! That's exactly how I feel!"

When that happens they will do anything you ask. Because anything you ask will be in alignment with what they already desire.

That's a deep well I just pushed you into! Follow it all the way down, and be rewarded with the cool fresh water of more sales, more often.

13

78-Year Old Bank Teller Foils Robbery

One Friday, a robber walks into a Wachovia bank branch in Allentown, PA. He intends to rob the place. He picks a 78-year old bank teller as his target. I guess he figured she would be a pushover.

Boy was he wrong.

Our Spunky Septuagenarian, whose name is Helen Roth, gave the robber a piece of her mind–but didn't give him ANY money.

She told him to scram, and that's what he did.

Here's the Million-Dollar Question

I wonder... if it was me, would I have done what Helen did? What about you?

Sometimes all we can do in a scary situation is the brave thing. That's what Helen did.

You know what? This danged recession is just like that robber. It wants to take our money unfairly. It already has taken some people's jobs and businesses.

But in my heart of hearts, I don't believe we need to give in. I think the WRONG ANSWER is to start shaking in our boots, handing over the money bags to Mr. Recession as if he were a gun-toting bank robber.

How to Deal With a Robber Named Recession

In today's world, you have a power never available in previous recessions–you have the Internet. You can start a new business on the Internet with less than $100.

There are dozens of ways to make a very good living online. Such as:

- Sell information (how-to guides, etc.)
- Sell services (web design, writing, programming, etc.)
- Open your own store in the world's biggest mall (eBay)
- Hang out your shingle as a consultant

And the list could be much longer, but you get the idea.

OR...You can save your EXISTING business using the power of the Internet. No traditional advertising required.

How? Just use some basic direct response techniques to give your business a "cash infusion." This is a bit more complex than the first option I mentioned, but there's plenty of information out there on the danged ol' Internet on how to do this. Much of it can be found on my own blog.

So what is my point? Simple. Stop trembling behind the counter. Stop making excuses:

- "I'm too old"...
- "It's not fair"...
- "I don't know what to do"...

Stop making excuses and just, if I may be permitted, have some guts.

If the recession is robbing YOU of sleep, peace of mind, or money... look that robber in the eye and say:

"Not today, Mister. Get outta here!"

Helen will applaud you. And so will I.

14

What the Heck Is "Laughter Yoga"?

Just when I thought I'd seen it all, I came across a website for something called "Laughter Yoga."

My first question was, "What the heck is 'laughter yoga'?"

Turns out it's exactly what it sounds like.

People get together in a yogaclass setting, and they LAUGH.

There's even a "Laughter Yoga Home Study" set, which is a bunch of DVDs that will set you back $195. I kid you not.

Now after a little Google research, I found out that doctors and patients say that this weird kind of yoga relieves stress and anxiety and could even strengthen the immune system.

It seems kind of like a stretch to me, but a lot of people swear by it and are willing to pay their hard-earned money for it. Just Google "laughter yoga" and you'll see what I'm talking about.

So what can we learn from this?

**Making money is simple if you remember that
all people really want is to FEEL BETTER.**

I mean, c'mon. If people will pay $195 to earn how to do "laughter yoga," doesn't that say a lot about what people really want?

How about diet books? We all know that most people who buy

diet books (or "get out of debt" books, or "get a better relationship" books, etc.) don't ever really lose weight (or get out of debt, or get a better relationship, etc.).

So why do they buy those books? TO FEEL BETTER!

The book makes them feel better about themselves. It makes them feel like they COULD go on the diet, or stick to a budget, or whatever.

Now, I think your product or service should provide real value, so that if your customers actually USED the product they would get the result.

But you should also think about making certain that your product itself provides a way to feel better.

Your marketing and sales material should absolutely make the prospects feel more positive, more focused, and more hopeful.

While I don't think any of us should be selling "false hope," I definitely feel we should be selling "hope," because hope makes people feel better, and that is ultimately what most human beings want.

15

Dead Men Don't Blog

If I died today, nobody would be able to log into my blog.

I've suddenly realized that is an important problem that could become an urgent one in the blink of an eye.

But wait. It gets worse. I own HUNDREDS of domain names, and have DOZENS of live, active websites. You can see that this multiplies my problem. Not only can nobody log into my blog, they also can't log into my other sites.

Obviously, as the title of this chapter intimates, "dead men don't blog." And they also don't market. Or Twitter. Or Facebook.

I've got some work to do, preparing for the inevitable day when my keyboard will go silent.

Why Am I Even Writing About This?

Well, I'm not being morbid. And I don't mean to depress you or weird you out. But I was reading a post over at Dave Winer's blog about how he's maintaining two online archives for relatives who have passed away.

Reading Dave's article on this subject made me realize...

1. **If I die** and want my work to live beyond the next hosting bill, I need to have a post-mortem plan for my blog.

2. **If I die** and DON'T want my work to live on, there needs to be a plan for how to get it OFF the web (some of my hosting is paid WAY in advance or is on auto-pay).

Regardless, I Need A Plan. And So Do You.

What about your sites?

Especially if you have a business (and even if you don't), you need to have a plan. At the very least, you could create a simple set of instructions and a list of your logins.

My plan, in case you're interested, includes the following steps:

1. **Create a list** of all my domain/blogs/hosting accounts login URLs and passwords.

2. **Specific instructions about** what needs to be done with each site.

3. **Create some "post-Ray"** emails that will let any readers or subscribers know what the status of the website is.

4. **Create instructions about** what to do with any merchant or payment systems that are set up for the sites.

That's just the rough draft of my plan, written on the fly. I'm sure I'll refine it. It'll take some time. But it will save someone (probably someone I love) a lot of work and frustration.

It is also good service to my readers and customers. What about you?

Do you have a "Dead Man Plan" for your websites?

16

How to Become a Superhero

You probably know who Clark Kent is. He's the fumbling, bumbling, mild-mannered newspaper reporter who wears the big geeky glasses.

He's a nice guy, but not exactly a great role-model for manhood. After all, we can ALL identify with Clark.

But when an emergency arises, Clark sheds the glasses and the business suit, revealing a being of extraordinary strength and power: Superman.

The Man of Steel. The "strange visitor from another planet who fights a never-ending battle for truth, justice, and the American way!"

You don't really need me to explain Superman to you. And that's the point of this chapter.

If you'd like to really amplify your marketing message, one of the best ways to do it is to become the superhero of choice for your prospects. Here's how you do that...

Identify the Villains Your Customers Face

These could be economic villains like rising interest rates, or psychological villains like poor self-esteem, or even health-related villains like arthritis.

Once you've identified the villain, get specific and identify the villain's superpowers and weapons.

Name Your Hero and His Powers

This could be you personally or your company–but you need to have a title or "superhero" name: something that sums up who you are and what you're about.

It should be short, catchy, and self-explanatory.

Clearly State Your Mission

Superman's mission statement is a great model: "Superman ... fights a never-ending battle for truth, justice, and the American way!"

Build your own mission statement–it should be short. Ideally one sentence like Superman's: more like a "slogan" than anything else.

A Real Life Example

THE VILLAIN: Anemic Advertising.

This creepy character sucks the life out of small business advertising budgets–by spending all your money on ads that get very little response.

Ad dollars go out, but revenue doesn't come in. It leaves victims penniless and discouraged. It destroys many businesses.

THE HERO: Captain Copywriter.

He magically transforms limp, lazy, lackluster ads into profit-pulling power- houses.

He multiplies revenue while at the SAME TIME slashes your ad spending.

He produces sales, profits, and peace of mind.

How to Become a Superhero

MISSION STATEMENT: "Captain Copywriter fights a never-ending battle for better ads, producing more profits, more often."

Use Your Identity

So how do you use your "superhero identity"?

Well, first of all, start "living it." If you were a copywriter who has now become Captain Copywriter – how would the Captain behave?

How would he talk? What would his costume (web site) look like?

Does he have an insignia? What are his sayings and catchphrases? (Superman had "Up, up and away!"–what would YOURS be?)

Even more important than all of this: once you start putting yourself into the state of mind of your "superhero character," you'll easily start thinking like he would think! Let me prove it.

If you came across a bank robbery in progress, you might not know what to do (other than maybe call the police).

But let's say you were Clark Kent and you came across that same robbery in progress. NOW what would you do?

You'd intervene, of course. You'd duck behind a door or into a hallway, put on your super-suit, and then move into action.

See how simply IMAGINING a superhero identity gives you access to superhero strategies?

The only thing you need to do is step into the ROLE of your business superhero... and then just ask yourself:

"What would Captain Copywriter do about this?"

And then work it out. What are you waiting for?

Take off those glasses, snap on that cape, and commence your crusade!

17

Simple But Not Easy

Not that long ago I was in the radio business. Luckily, I saw the handwriting on the wall that told me radio was in big trouble.

I began running around telling all my radio comrades that we needed to change the way we did business or we were going to be in big trouble.

Of course, they didn't want to hear that–so they didn't change. In fact, I was told my fears were silly: iPods and satellite radio and the Internet were no threat to radio at all. That's what my corporate bosses told me, anyway.

When I tried to explain that it wasn't fear that was motivating me, but rather the recognition of a trend that was inevitable... well, some of them laughed.

They're not laughing any more

I've been out of the radio business for several years now, but hardly a week goes by that one of my old comrades doesn't call me and tell me how the margins are continuing to shrink, listenership continues to drop like a lead balloon, and corporate failures and layoffs are coming at an ever-increasing rate of speed.

There is good news in all this

Radio's answer is a simple one... but not easy. It's the same answer I was touting years ago when I decided to get out that game altogether:

Make a better product!

So what does that look like for the radio industry?

- Pay the expense to hire good talent–and let them make radio shows that are compelling and entertaining.

- Stop playing so many commercials (in fact, I suggest you stop playing any commercials and invent a new revenue model. I'm sure that idea is too scary for radio folks to even contemplate.)

- Decide you're in it for the long haul, and stop managing to next week's "revenue number."

- Forget the ratings game and focus on the results you get for your clients instead.

- Serve the community you operate in with real community service, not the usual "lip service."

That ought to get you started, radio folks. This also applies to almost every other suffering business or industry.

You probably already know what you need to do. The problem is, it's simple... but it's not easy.

18

Mint.com, the "iPad" Business Lesson, and Toyota

Mint.com makes everything about monitoring and managing your finances super easy.

The site is a marvel of simplicity: simple copy, simple navigation, and simple user interface.

What's amazing is: the conceptual "sale" they have to make is complex to get you to share your financial information with them, which is necessary for their site to be of any real use to you.

They have to overcome a very rational fear on the part of their prospect: "Why should I give these guys all my passwords? What will they do with that information?"

Add to that the following complexity… after they've convinced you to give up all your usernames and passwords for all your financial accounts, then they have to interact with all those other websites to aggregate the data into a very user-friendly online "dashboard" of your finances.

It all appears very simple to the end user, but it is very hard to do. And they appear to be making a fortune.

So how does one do such a thing?

1. **First, lots of** thinking and planning.

2. **Then lots of** hard work.

3. **Make a big** investment in infrastructure and programming.

4. **Take a huge** risk that it will all work.

5. **Spend time and** thought on marketing that is smart, effective... and simple.

Probably not what most entrepreneurs want to hear–especially the part about "thinking and planning" and "lots of hard work." but that's how you make a Mint (.com).

The "iPad" Business Lesson

Stop offering so many options.

What is the iPad? It's essentially a stripped-down MacBook Pro. No keyboard, no optical drive, and a smaller screen.

The iPad does only what most people actually do with their Apple laptop: email, surf the web, play games, listen to music, or watch movies.

No, it's not the ideal machine for writing a novel or editing video. But that's just the point.

If you realize that most people do only a few things with their laptop... and you realize you can eliminate expensive things like the keyboard and optical drive... you can simplify the device.

You can make it cheaper. You can sell more of them. And you can make more money – by offering fewer options and features.

The Toyota Effect

Why do you believe what you believe? How often do you stop to consider that question?

Mint.com, the "iPad" Business Lesson, and Toyota

For decades, a majority of American car buyers thought Toyota made the highest quality and safest cars for the money.

What do you suppose the majority of American car buyers think about Toyota cars right about now? Toyota is an option.

Key question: what caused the change?

The easy answer is that recalls caused the change. A more sophisticated answer is the news coverage of the recalls caused the change.

Neither of those answers recognizes the deeper lesson:

Management (or mismanagement) of how and when a story is told powerfully influences the stories we believe and tell ourselves.

How many of your beliefs did you choose consciously?

19

3 Keys to Instantly Make Your Business More Effective

1) Your Last Project

You've heard the exercise: "If you only had 1 week left to live, how would you spend it?"

I've always found this an instructive thought experiment – and also a little vague.

Here's a refinement:

> **What if you only had 1 project left to work on?**

- Which project would you choose?
- How would you go about it?
- What would be your criteria for success?

My guess is the answers to these questions will be different than the way you've been approaching your projects up until now.

My question is: will that continue to be the case? What if you approached every project (business, personal, or any other category) as if it were your last?

2) Customer Selection Determines Quality of Life

This is hard for a lot of folks to swallow, but it's true anyway.

Instead of scrambling madly for any customer who will hand you money, be selective.

Determine what kind of customer you don't want to deal with, and work hard to exclude those customers from your business.

If you are brave and decide to take this step you will find:

- You get more customers you like doing business with.
- Your customers will spend more on each transaction.
- Your customers will come back more often.
- You will make more money.
- You will work less, not more.

That sounds good, yes? It's made a world of difference for me.

Go thou and do likewise.

3) The Answer to Every Marketing Problem

Does the guy selling beer at the baseball stadium have a marketing problem? Does Disney have trouble marketing umbrellas at their theme park during Florida's legendary afternoon thundershowers?

How about fireworks dealers right before the Fourth of July?

None of these situations present a marketing problem, because people already want the product.

The product, in other words, sells itself. This can happen by design, in any business. You simply have to use your "thinker" to find the hidden opportunities in your business.

For instance, Disney had a problem with their Florida theme parks. They hadn't counted on the fact that it rains in Florida A LOT.

This problem was an opportunity in disguise, because someone realized the most valued commodity in a rainstorm is an umbrella.

And so now when it starts to rain in the Magic Kingdom, there's a parade, all the "cast members" talk about the "liquid sunshine," and the umbrellas come out from the back of the store to the front. And they sell themselves.

What opportunities exist in your business that would allow you to sell products that prospects don't have to be persuaded to buy? Think about that. Answer it, do something about it – and prosper.

20

"It Is What It Is": How to Handle Problems

The first step to solving a problem is: acknowledge you have one.

Life is full of stuff we don't like: car accidents, business bankruptcies, illness, divorce, war, crime, etc.

Being in business carries its own seemingly endless catalog of potential problems. Yeah, I call 'em problems and not "challenges"... because they are problems. Keep reading. All will become clear.

Pretending that these problems don't exist or that they don't change things, is folly. It's irresponsible.

In the business world, lots of people like to yammer on about how much they love Napoleon Hill's *Think and Grow Rich*.

Whenever I hear people praising that book, most of them neglect one of the points Hill made: the importance of accurate thinking.

Accurate thinking involves accepting reality, whether you like it or not.

Instead of engaging in "positive thinking" and denying the reality of your situation, start by thinking accurately about what has really happened.

As my friend Armand Morin says, "It is what it is."

Too many times we try to put a "positive spin" on things, thinking we will somehow make things better if we simply don't admit things are what they are.

Now, I am not saying you should dwell on the problem. I'm not suggesting you live in the Land of Eternal Pessimism (I am an optimist, through and through).

The trick is to spend about 10% of your time accurately assessing and appreciating the scope of whatever problem you are facing, whether it be business trouble, relationship problems, illness, or what have you. Then spend 90% of your time focusing on how to make it better.

Living in denial will not make things better and neither will living in the Land of Eternal Pessimism.

Only accurate thinking equips you to really deal with whatever life throws your way. It's not always comfortable. But it is always the best wisdom.

The next time life throws you a problem, please don't put on the Helmet of Denial. Instead, put on your big-boy face, look at that problem with your eyes wide open, and say, "It is what it is."

And then ask, "So what am I going to do about it?"

21

7 Stupid Ways to Define Success

Here are 7 ways to define success that are guaranteed to make you feel like crap:

1. Your bank balance.
2. How fancy your car is.
3. How fancy your house is.
4. How fancy your clothes are.
5. The shape of your body.
6. How other people see you.
7. How popular you are.

Here is a definition of success that, if you believe and practice it, will allow you to feel great (and be great)... no matter what your external circumstances might be:

"Success is the progressive realization of a worthy goal or ideal."- Earl Nightingale

(Hint: the key words are "progressive" and "worthy".)

22

The A-Team School of Marketing

Have you seen the A-Team movie? I did – twice!

For those who don't know, it's a remake of the old TV show, and it's about an elite group of Army Rangers who "specialize in the impossible."

The unit – called an "Alpha Unit" or "A-Team" – is led by Colonel Hannibal Smith. And Hannibal has some trademark wisdom that allows his team to accomplish the impossible; it's wisdom that works for marketers, too.

Here are his three gems of wisdom:

1. "No matter how random things appear, there's always a plan."

Seems like just when things get darkest for the A-Team, that's when Hannibal's plan unfolds like clockwork. And it's a thing of beauty to behold.

Marketers are well-advised to have a plan of attack, especially in this sometimes perilous New Economy.

Do YOU have a plan?

Or are you just "faking it," making it up as you go along?

2. "Give me a minute, I'm good. Give me an hour, we're great. Give me six months and I'm unbeatable."

Hannibal knows the value of time well spent in planning, in research- and given enough time, knows he can't be beaten.

When the chips are down, do you have the confidence mindset that there is always a solution to any marketing problem, given enough time?

3. "I love it when a plan comes together."

Hannibal's greatest joy seems to be his crazy plans coming to fruition.

This is something every marketer should be able to relate to! If you need a shot of inspiration for your business, you could do worse than going to the movies and watching the A-Team in action!

23

3 Lies That Hold You Back

There's not much holding you back other than your own thinking.

Our culture is replete with stories of people who had every disadvantage yet succeeded wildly – and that not through luck but through focused effort.

Submitted as proof: Ray Charles, Stephen Hawking, and Helen Keller

So what is it about our thinking that so often holds us back, especially when we have no great physical disadvantage?

Note: the aforementioned cases preclude any healthy person from excuse-making... and they also demonstrate that what I'm about to say applies even to those who are blind, deaf, or crippled.

Here are three lies that hold you back. Escape these lies, and escape the limitations you've imposed on yourself.

1. **The past equals the future.** The perfect lie for convincing you to not even try anything, since it's "never worked in the past."

2. **Good thing Thomas Edison**, the Wright Brothers, and Abraham Lincoln didn't buy this lie.

3. **Ready, Aim, Fire.** Sounds like good wisdom, until you realize most get stuck on "Aim," so that it ends up being "Ready, Aim... Aim... Aim... Aim..."

4. **Proven methods are safest.** Maybe they are, but if we relied only on "proven methods," we'd have no space shuttle, no antibiotics, no Apple computer, and no polio vaccine.

There are, of course, many other lies that hold people back.

What lies are you believing that bar you from greatness?

Believing a lie means you are, in a sense, partnering with a liar. Think about it. And then do something about it!

24

How to Write a Book in 7 Days

One of the very best ways to establish your authority in a given field is to write a book about it.

After all, when we want to acknowledge someone as a bona fide expert, one of the figures of speech we use is "they wrote the book" on that subject. Meaning: they know all there is to know about it.

Writing a book seems like a lot of work.

It doesn't have to be. If you really know your topic well, you could probably complete your first draft in a week.

Here's a simple plan for writing a book:

"Prep Day" – Day ZERO:

Come up with your title. Something like "The Insider's Secrets of Raising Chinchillas" (or whatever your topic is).

Then write an outline of what you want to say about your topic: 7 main subjects (chapters) with 3 points about each chapter.

Sample:

"The Insider's Secrets of Raising Chinchillas"

- **Chapter 1:** Why Raising Chinchillas Is a Great Business
- **Chapter 2:** The Facts About the Chinchilla Business
- **Chapter 3:** What Other Chinchilla Ranchers Have to Say About It
- **Chapter 4:** My Personal Chinchilla Story ...and so on, for 7 "Chapters"

Then, you keep going...

- **Day 1:** Record yourself just talking through your outline of Chapters 1 & 2.
- **Day 2:** Record yourself just talking through Chapters 3 & 4.
- **Day 3**: Record yourself just talking through Chapters 5 & 6.
- **Day 4:** Record yourself just talking through Chapter 7 ... and a short talk on "About this book" that will serve as the book's "Introduction." It's best to do this after you have finished dictation of the whole book. You'll have a better idea what to say.
- **Day 5:** Send off your audios for transcription. Use someone who will "clean up" all your stumbles and false starts, etc.
- **Day 6:** Do nothing.
- **Day 7:** Receive your transcriptions back. You now have a first draft of your book.

The average person, speaking at a normal pace, will dictate about 20 pages per hour. That's 140 pages in 7 hours (1 hour per chapter).

After editing, that will be about 120 pages – a good length for a non-fiction book.

Depending on the transcription service you use, they may take longer than two days to turn all this around. But your part is done on Day 4!

That's it – you've written a book in less than a week

You could even hire someone to polish your first draft into a final draft. That should take a good writer no more than a couple of weeks.

In less than one month from today, you could have your own, original, 120-page book. That will make you the expert who "wrote the book" on your topic.

While it took me considerably longer than a week... I do believe in the value of publishing one's own, real books.

My book, *Writing Riches*, is available on Amazon.

25

What Were You Put Here to Do?

I believe you were created to do great things.

I believe every one of us was endowed by our Creator not only with "rights" but also with "potential."

And I believe part of our mission here on Planet Earth is to unlock that little mystery box and enjoy the potentials that have been embedded inside us.

You may ask, "If we were created with that potential, why does it have to be a mystery?" Because that's what makes it fun. Believe it or not.

So... your homework for today...
Start working on your own "mystery box":
What were you sent here to do?

If you don't believe all that stuff about being "sent here" to do something, just pretend:

What if you WERE sent here to do something? What would it be?

And what on earth could be more important than (a) figuring that out and (b) DOING it?

If you think this has nothing to do with business... well, you're just not thinkin' hard enough.

26

BS Excuses That Kill Greatness

One of the things that kinda gets under my skin is the "BS Excuses" people use to explain why they can't do things.

Now I'm not saying we don't sometimes just have a tough go of it. We all do from time to time. I'm talking about "loser's limp"... where you start limping early in the race just so you can later explain why you lost.

Some language that's a sure tip-off that you've wandered into the "Land of BS Excuses"...

- "There are just no jobs/clients/opportunities in this market/niche/city ..."

That's funny.

What are all those people doing on the freeway every day at 9 am if they're not going to WORK?

Or how do so many new businesses start every month if there are no clients?

- "There's no room for the little guy in this company/town/Industry."

Just Get Started

People were spouting this SAME BS when Steve Jobs and his pal Woz started a little company named Apple Computer out of a garage.

It's just as much BS now as it was then.

- "The government has killed this market/business/country."

The government interfering in business is not NEWS... it's part of doing business! And plenty of businesses make a profit despite that fact. Get over it!

- "People are just not buying cars/ boats/ books/ airplanes/ swimming pools these days."

Ummm.... BS! In fact, DOUBLE BS! They ARE buying all these things and more... and I've seen plenty of data showing the sale of LUXURY items are UP lately.

Just because they're not buying from YOU does not mean they are not BUYING.

- "Long sales copy doesn't work any more." or "I can't write sales copy."

All you have to do is get a good course on the subject.

For example: my own course http://webcopywritingexplained.com for copywriters. Just "follow the instructions" to copy that will sell your stuff for you.

If you suspect that you even occasionally engage in any of this "BS Excuse" nonsense...

I hereby challenge you to Ten Days of Zero BS Excuse-Making.

Here's how to play: for the next 10 days just don't make a single BS excuse about anything in your life.

If you mess up on, say, Day 3... reset the clock and start over at Day 1. I warn you, it may take you a while to get all the way to 10 days. But once you have, I can almost guarantee:

BS Excuses That Kill Greatness

1. **Your results in** whatever it is you do will have improved because you will have taken away your biggest impediment–your own EXCUSES.

2. **You will never** want to go back to your old, excuse-making ways.

3. **Are you in?**

27

Tonight, We Try to Take Over the World

In the vein of thinking big, I've been working on a new TOTW plan.

TOTW stands for "Take Over The World."

I won't go into the details about that plan. It's big, complex, and multi-faceted... but none of that is really relevant to the point I want to make.

What I do want to talk about is why TOTW plans so often go astray.

It's simple really... they're either too big or too small

It's pretty much that simple. And I learned it from Pinky & the Brain. In case you don't remember the old animated cartoon, it was about two genetically enhanced laboratory mice.

Brain is the schemer.

Pinky is the good-natured but feebleminded member of the duo. The opening song of each episode is preceded by this dialogue:

Pinky: "Gee, Brain, what do you want to do tonight?"

The Brain: "The same thing we do every night,

Pinky—try to take over the world!"

Every one of Brain's plans end in failure – either because the plan was just impossible (too big) or because Pinky's idiocy screwed it up.

So what does this have to do with you and me? Lots.

The magic of thinking big is in knowing what kind of big thinking actually works:

Think Big but Not Impossible:

Don't limit yourself, but be accurate in your thinking.

For instance, if you're doing your very first product launch, it is probably not accurate to think you're going to crack the million dollar mark (unless you have accurate facts to the contrary).

Don't Do Stupid Stuff:

We all know when we're doing something stupid, most of the time.

But just as a guideline: if it's disrespectful of people, if it's less than your best, or if it smacks of moral ambiguity... it's probably stupid.

Don't do it.

Okay, now that you and I have those details cleared up... you know what we're doing, right? The same thing we do every day—try to take over the world!

28

5 Fundamentals of Bulletproof Business Profits

Some people view starting or running a business as "risky," but you can manage the risks.

The ones that scare people the most are the easiest to manage.

Here are 5 fundamentals that will help you bulletproof your profits. The temptation will be to dismiss them because they're so simple. That would be a big mistake.

1. **Find a large** group of people who are crazy about something and are already spending money on it.

2. **Find out what** that group of people wants in the something that they buy – either the "something better" that they want (improvement) or the "something NEXT" that they want (innovation).

3. **Make the thing** they want. And make it crazy good.

4. **Make all your** advertising trackable, and only do direct response advertising where you ask for the sale and you give them a specific instruction / opportunity to buy.

5. **Notice what works** and do that more; notice what doesn't and stop doing that.

These aren't the only fundamentals. Just 5 that I think are an important starting point.

29

Strength: the Secret Power of Achievement

Most people know what to do; they just don't do what they know.

This is why so many fail to achieve success with their business, with their weightloss program, with quitting smoking or just about anything that requires discipline.

Here's the rub: achievement requires discipline.

Discipline is not the magic ingredient of achievement; however, the strength of discipline is required if achievement is to be sustained.

Strength in discipline cannot be faked. This is where people get stuck. As Warren Buffet said:

> **"When the tide goes out it's easy to see who was skinny dipping."**

In life, the "tide goes out" whenever we start pushing against resistance. Pushing against a heavy weight is how we build strength in our muscles, and we build that strength by pushing against the weight on a regular basis.

If we have not been meeting resistance on a regular, consciously created, and purposely planned basis, we won't be able to move the weight when it's crucial to do so.

When it comes to achievement, the same principles apply:

Achievement flows from discipline, which requires strength.

Here's the part that makes this all seem a mystery to most: strength on the outside only comes after you develop strength on the inside.

Mental strength comes first. Take every thought captive and make each one serve your purpose. This is the genesis of achievement.

30

7 Effortless Productivity Tips

Okay, let me 'fess up... nothing in life is truly "effortless" – even breathing takes some effort. But these 7 tips are guaranteed to ramp up your productivity and they take very little effort. At least that's been true for me.

1. Have a morning routine that sets you up for success.

>Mine is summed up in this weird little mnemonic: WWW-B-PREP (which stands for Wake, Water, Walk, Bible, Pray, Eat, Plan). It takes me about 90 minutes to complete and makes my day a "win" first thing.
>Your routine could be much simpler. I share mine because it's an example that is real.

2. Get at least one block of "focus time."

>This is a block of time where you work on your most important, profitable activity of the day, before you check email or voicemail.

3. Use a digital timer to limit your time surfing the Internet or "working" on your social media presence.

Don't let this time waster rule your time.

4. Don't take incoming calls.

Screen them using voicemail.

5. Return calls in one block of time each day.

Most things are not emergencies, and once a day is enough.

6. Return emails in one block of time each day.

See #5.

7. Keep your "to-do" lists in a context form:

In other words, have different lists of things that can only be completed in a specific context.

For example, have an "Errands" list of things you can do when you're out and about; have a "Phone" list of all the people you need to call (with numbers) for those times when you have the energy and time to make calls; have an "Internet" list of things you can only do when you're online.

You'll never wonder what to do in any given context once you have these lists.

For more on this, get David Allen's book, *Getting Things Done*.

31

The Inception Guide to Marketing

If you haven't seen the film Inception yet, don't worry–there are no spoilers here. But there's an important lesson in the movie for marketers and evangelists alike.

In the film, Cobb (played by Leonardo DiCaprio) is talking about the act of "inception": planting an idea in another person's mind.

Here's what Cobb says:

> "What's the most resilient parasite? An idea. A single idea from the human mind can build cities. An idea can transform the world and rewrite all the rules."

What this means to marketers or to anyone who wants to spread their ideas should be obvious.

Once you have planted an idea in the minds of your audience, it's very, very difficult for that idea to be dislodged.

This is why, for example, in a courtroom there is an advantage to telling your side of the story first. The weight of the idea you planted in the jury's mind is hard for your opponent to overcome.

The more powerfully and indelibly you can imprint your idea on a large number of minds, the more influence you have.

This is the "secret" behind clichés, stereotypes, and proverbs.

For instance, the advice "look before you leap" is a powerful way of simply and briefly summing up a powerful idea, and that maxim influences many of us when we are about to make a crucial decision.

The only way to counteract a powerful idea like "look before you leap" is with another idea just as powerful: "he who hesitates is lost."

Your goal as a marketer should be to plant your ideas early and often. Here's how:

1. **Formulate your idea** simply and memorably.

Examples: "DeliveringHappiness," "GettingThingsDone," "Unleashing the IdeaVirus."

2. **Put your idea** into distributable form.

3. **Encourage the free** and massive distribution of your idea.

I know... the question burning in your mind is, "But how do I make money doing that?" Good question – with many answers.

You make money explaining the idea. No matter how simple it is, people will always want you to explain it, and they will pay you to do so.

You've told people what to do (your idea) – now tell them how to do it and charge them.

Leverage the Authority gained from spreading the idea into other, profitable jobs, gigs, and businesses.

32

Get Instant Value From Your Dusty Old Info-Products

So you've got all these info-products you've bought but never used. Some of them you've never freaking OPENED.

Here's way to get back ALL the money you've invested... and feel immensely good about yourself. This is also a way to recoup your losses if you've gotten caught on the latest guru product treadmill.

They're only losses if you fail to do something with them.

You'll need a couple of hours depending on how bad your "habit" is. You'll also need a legal pad and a pen.

Got all your school supplies? Good. Here's what you do:

1. Start with the info-product on top of the pile.

Open it and look for the "Quick Start Guide," or better yet, one of those nifty "Cheat Sheets" or "Checklists" they so often come with.

2. Go through the Quickstart Guide, or Checklist, or Manual, or (heaven forbid) the actual DVD or CD labeled #1.

Find the FIRST action item you can locate from this particular info-product. Doesn't matter how small, just find one item you can DO.

Ideally it would be a short something like changing a headline, setting up a new squeeze page, or setting up a survey that you can do in a few minutes.

The only rule is: it must be something you can do in ONE SITTING.

3. Got your first action item? Write it down on your legal pad.

4. Now put away info-product one.

Put it neatly back on its shelf. Move on to info-product #2 and repeat until you've gone through the whole pile.

When you're done you should have a good list of things to do, each of which can be done in just one sitting.

Now – and I mean NOW – schedule a time on your calendar when you will sit down and do ALL these items. The very best scenario is: do them right now.

The most important thing is: complete your list in 3 days or less. Do NOT let it sit around longer than that.

If you'll do this exercise, I guarantee three things:

1. **You will have** gotten all your value from those info-products; everything else in there that you act on is just "gravy."

2. **You will have** done more than 99.9% of all info-product buyers will EVER do.

3. **You'll see a** surge in your results AND you'll have an immediate boost in your self-esteem.

Try it and see.

33

There Are No Secrets

As much as I have used the word "secrets" in my own marketing, I guess I should be embarrassed to tell you this, but...

There are no real secrets. Just information you don't have.
The big PILLARS of success in any business are simple and clear:

1. Find that group of passionate people

2. Find out what they want

3. Make what they want

4. Sell it to them

And as long as you do that, you'll make money.

Now, are there refinements? Are there little tricks, tweaks, and tactics that can get you where you want to go... FASTER? Yes. But those aren't secrets.

You can get access to the information, either free, although sometimes time-consuming, or for pay, which is sometimes the best way to go and FASTER.

Still, no matter how you get the needed information, it's not "secret"... it's just information you don't yet have.

34

Marketing by Number

We live by the calendar. Our year is marked by signposts. Dates on the calendar around which we plan our annual journey. In the USA, some of the major calendar signposts include:

- New Year's Day
- Super Bowl Sunday
- Valentine's Day
- St. Patrick's Day
- Easter
- Memorial Day
- Mother's Day
- Father's Day
- Independence Day
- Back to School
- Labor Day
- Halloween
- Veterans Day
- Thanksgiving
- Christmas

There are many others, of course, and your list will vary depending on your cultural and religious background.

The point is: the major signposts are easy to identify. Easy to construct a marketing calendar around.

What's the point of that? We copywriters talk a lot about "joining the conversation already taking place in the prospect's mind" (a phrase borrowed from Robert Collier).

When you tie your marketing efforts to major mindset-changing calendar dates, you go a long way toward "joining" that conversation.

John E. Kennedy identified the power of "reason why" copy: prospects are more likely to respond if you give them a reason why they should.

They're more likely to pay attention to your promotion if you give them a "reason why" you're doing the promotion to begin with.

Retailers have done this so long and with so little imagination, we've grown accustomed to it.

"The January White Sale"...

"The Sweetheart Sale" for Valentine's Day...

"Saving the Green" sales for St. Patrick's Day...

The good news for your online business is that all of these "old school" ideas work very well online. If you can get a little more creative with them (for instance, having a "Click Your Treat" promotion around Halloween) they work even better.

The point is: give your prospects and customers a new reason to visit your website at least once per month.

Planning your promotional calendar becomes very easy when you adopt this model.

The list above is not a bad start. If you're more ambitious, you can select from hundreds of "reasons why" by looking through a holidays and observances calendar ... and have a reason to do a promotion 52 times per year.

Need ideas about what sort of promotions to do? Borrow ideas from the businesses that have made an art form of this method: brick & mortar retailers such as car dealers, big box stores, and grocery stores in particular will supply you with a rich "swipe file" of ideas.

Just visit your local library (yes, they still exist) and get the back issues of your local newspaper's Sunday issues. They will have the most ads for the last year.

You'll have 52 "mini-swipe files" to build your library of promotions from.

What do you suppose might happen to your sales and profits then?

35

Are Your Internet Business Goals Too High?

I was on the phone with 'Jack' because he's one of my subscribers. He sent me an email saying his back was to the wall.

"I just don't think I can make a living online," said Jack.

He had been trying and trying to make this "online business thing" work, and had spent thousands of dollars over the last year or so.

He had only made about $200 to show for all his efforts. Jack was ready to give up.

"Jack," I said, "if you're willing to listen, I think I can help."

"I'm ready to try anything," he said.

(I smiled.)

"And that is your first problem," I answered...which led me to the reason for writing this chapter.

Maybe you're not in Jack's situation. Maybe you're not desperate, but I know that a lot of people are asking the same questions as Jack.

Among those questions:

- Can I really make a living online and quit my day job?

- If I put in all this effort and work, will I make money?

- Am I being ripped off by people who sell me all this "make money" stuff on the Internet?

- Are there secrets being held back that I don't know about?

My best answer is the same one I gave to Jack: "Yes, you can make a living online...and yes, you are probably wasting some money right now."

The good news is, if you'd start taking the right actions, you could turn it all around in just a day or two.

Here's what I mean. Most people struggling to build an online business are too busy buying the latest "system" or "course" or "software" or "service"...too busy BUYING stuff to ever MAKE any money.

For these people, their primary online "business" activity consists of evaluating their next purchase! Think about it.

How much time do you spend reading sales letters or reviews of products, courses, and seminars? How much time do you spend reading and posting in online forums, discussing the merits of this or that new program? And once you buy that new "thing"–whatever it is–how far do you get with it?

Do you have any big courses sitting on a shelf that you haven't finished yet? Haven't watched all the DVDs or listened to all the audios? How about courses that you did watch all of and got all excited by...but didn't follow through with all the STEPS?

Be honest. It's just you and me here. My guess is that this line of thinking leaves you a bit uncomfortable.

Don't worry–I think we're all at least a little bit "guilty" of this syndrome, but there is a solution, and I'm going to offer you three steps that may help you finally get your business "off the ground."

The same three suggestions I offered to Jack.

Action Step 1: Set an Achievable Short-Term Goal.

We spend too much time trying to figure out how to achieve some huge goal, like "make $10,000 a month."

Are Your Internet Business Goals Too High?

Set a more achievable, short-range goal. For instance, why not just shoot for $500? Once you make $500 online, you can work on increasing it, right?

The power in this is simple: once you MAKE that $500, you have a lot more BELIEF that you can do it again...and again...and again. There is REAL power in that belief. If $500 seems out of reach for you, then just set a goal you CAN believe in. Even if it's only $100.

On the other hand, there are those reading this letter who are already making $10,000 or $20,000 per month...you'll need a bigger goal, but the principle is the same no matter where you are.

Action Step 2: Pick a Tactic for Achieving That Goal

Notice I didn't say pick a "strategy." That's because if you're struggling to get your business off the ground, "strategy" may be too big for you to tackle right now.

What you need is one effective "tactic": a specific set of actions you can take to achieve your objective.

For instance, if you want to build a list of subscribers, one tactic to use is to post in forums to drive traffic to your "squeeze page" (a forced opt-in page used to get subscribers). Make your posts helpful and informative, and put the link to your "squeeze page" in the signature block.

If you work at the above tactic diligently, you WILL start seeing subscribers signing up for your list within a few short days.

There are many other tactics you might choose; I only offer this one as an example. There are lots of tactics that do, in fact, work.

Your problem is likely not a lack of good ideas for tactics. It's that you have too many good ideas and can't focus on any one of them! Which leads us to...

Action Step 3: Stick with It Until You Achieve the Goal

Too often, I see people get started with a tactic they're excited about–only to watch them give up on it too early. Stay with your tactic.

Notice what works. Notice what doesn't.

Adjust your approach accordingly–but stick it out until you've made your $500 (or whatever your goal was). Until that time, keep blinders on.

Ignore all the other offers, emails, and attractive "tactics of the week" that come along.

Just focus on YOUR chosen tactic until you have that $500!

Then What Do You Do?

Once you've achieved your goal, you'll be faced with a decision: what do you do next?

Do you keep at it, employ the same tactic for the next $500? Maybe. That choice will be up to you.

Keep this in mind: what you will have learned from this exercise is vital. You will have proven to yourself that:

1. You can make money with your online business.

2. You can achieve a goal you set for yourself.

3. And you know at least one tactic for doing it.

Don't you think the next step will seem just a little bit easier now?

I hope that if you, like Jack, have been wondering whether you can "really" make it in your online business, you will take this message to heart and at least give my suggestions a shot.

36

3 Little Marketing Moves That Make More Money

If you're looking to make more money in your business, and you'd like to do that immediately, it may take less work than you think.

You've heard the saying that "little hinges swing the doors." Perhaps you've heard it so often that the profundity of that saying has been lost on you.

The fact is, small actions can lead to big results, and consciously chosen small actions can lead to enormous results.

Here are three little "marketing moves" that can enrich your profits almost immediately, when performed correctly. Please do not dismiss them based on their simplicity; their power springs from their simplicity.

1. Call your customers on the phone.

It's great if you have a script developed for this, but even if you don't... call them anyway.

Simply calling a large number of your customers and asking, "How are things going? Is there anything we can do to help?" will often lead to new business and sales, even though that wasn't the overt intention of your call.

If you don't get results with this technique... you haven't called enough people.

2. Send your customers mail.

Some people don't answer the phone or don't respond well to phone calls. No problem.

Send a piece of mail to your customers. It doesn't even have to be a piece of mail with an offer, although that's probably the best piece of mail to send.

The problem with sending mail that makes an offer is most people will do it wrong. Most people will make it look so much like an ad that it will end up in the trash can.

Here's an alternative: send a one-page letter, hand-addressed and hand-signed, that says something like:

> **"How are things going? Is there anything we can do to help? Here's our phone number–please call...".**

Don't laugh. Some people will call. And the ones who do are your best prospects.

3. Ask for referrals.

Call up your current customers, and ask them if they feel you're doing a good job for them.

Most of them, presumably, will say yes. If that's the case, ask them, "Who else can you think of who might benefit from our help?" Maybe even give them suggestions to help jog their memory.

If done correctly, simply asking for referrals will get you new business. The fact is, almost nobody does this. Prove it to yourself: when was the last time you asked for a referral?

There you go. Three little marketing moves that can put money in your bank account almost immediately.

37

What To Do Next

I bet you can see this one coming from a mile way.

Now that you've read this book, picked up some tips, and probably have at least a few ideas you'd like to try - it's time to...

Just get started.

In fact, I'd like to issue a two-part challenge to you.

Challenge Part One

Take one idea from this book and start the implementation of that idea in the next 2 minutes. Obviously, you'll have to pick something that can be started in 2 minutes. But don't get too caught up in completing this task, just get it started.

That could possibly look like:

- Sending an email to a customer.

- Calling a new vendor to start a dialog.

- Assigning a new project to one of your staff.

- Or even scheduling a brainstorming session on things you can "just get started."

There are a limitless number of possibilities. Just pick one and then do it.

It's that simple.

Challenge Part Two

The next challenge is a little more involved, but the potential payoff is huge.

Take some time (perhaps in that brainstorming session you just scheduled) to come up with 21 ideas for projects or processes you can "just get started". Then schedule one of them each day for the next 21 business days on your calendar.

Follow through on this list, and actually start each project or process on the assigned day.

If you do this, 21 business days from now you may find your business has been revolutionized for the better. You will certainly see more life and activity in your business than you likely have seen in a very long time.

Okay, I've issued the challenges. Do you accept?

Good.

Then you know what comes next.

~Just Get Started~

How to Contact Ray

If you are interested in online business, marketing, copywriting, and how to be a follower of Jesus in the marketplace, Ray can help. For more information about keynotes and workshops, contact Ray Edwards International, Inc.:

    Phone: (509) 624-2220
    Email: info@RayEdwards.com
    Online: www.RayEdwards.com

    Ray Edwards International, Inc
    2910 E 57th Ave Ste 5 #330
    Spokane, WA 99223

Sign-up for Ray Edwards' email newsletter at:

    www.RayEdwards.com

To purchase bulk copies of this book at a discount for your customers, or for your organization, please contact Ray Edwards International, Inc.:

    specialsales@RayEdwards.com or (509) 624-2220

www.ingramcontent.com/pod-product-compliance
Lightning Source LLC
Chambersburg PA
CBHW051541170526
45165CB00002B/829